This book belongs to

First Edition 2012

Library of Congress Control Number: 2012915490

Summary: A young boy on a baseball team learns that his best coaches in life are his parents.

ISBN # 978-0-9882214-0-6
Printed in China
CPSIA Section 103 Compliant
www.beaconstar.com/consumer
ID: M0120603. Tracking No.: M308780-1-9071

The artwork was created with watercolor.
Book design by David Vilardi

# Your Best Coaches

## by Louisa Luisi

### Illustrated by Kika Esteves

# As you grow up, it will seem

that you are on a
winning baseball team.

When you are standing at the plate,
staring at the ace,

the catcher will be ready for the
ball to meet his glove's embrace.

You will be nervous,
heart pounding with fear,

knowing you may strike out when the ball comes near.

But your coaches will be watching, rooting for you,

hoping you hit the ball
and make it through.

They will stand behind you,
whether a grand slam or strikeout,

knowing you have
played your best
without any doubt.

# You can hit it to the outfield or a slow ground ball

and your coaches will see you as the greatest player of all.

They will be there
when you are
thrown a curve

because your Mommy
and Daddy are the best
coaches there are.

I dedicate this book to my best coaches,
my mom and dad.

This book would not have been possible
without generous funding from

David Vilardi • The Famularo Family • Giacomo's Italian Market • The Lombardi Family

A very special thanks to

Agnese Irwin • Amy Davidson • Anna and Francesco Luisi • Bill Dimodugno • Cindy and Mike Gagliardi •
Damien Hirsch • David M. Siwy • Diana Price • Donna M. Lyons • Doug Aday, Jr. • Eileen and Matt D'Elia •
Everett E. Robinson, IV • Gina and Steven Vilardi • Grandpop John K. Moss • Hannah Cohan • Jabber •
James Kleimann • Jason J. Consoli • Jessica and Brian Zorger • Jessica Stroebel • John Judge •
Kathy and Marshall Suarez • Kim Schaye • Kim, Mike, Brittany, Anthony, and Nicholas Vilardi •
Kristen and Thomas Shanley • Leslie Milton and Emma Rosenthal • Liz, Gary, Emilie, and Julia Louizides •
Mari and Hayro Bekarian • Maria and Todd Aiello • Marie Rufrano-Wilson and Phil Wilson •
Marta, Felix, Francesco, Matthew, and Giuliana Luisi • Marysol and Patrick Duffy • Matt Cheplic •
Maureen • Meg Schaefer and Steve Katter • Michael Halwagy • Michael Yevchak • Nancy and Joe Scanlon •
Nikomeh Anderson • Paul Bednardz • Paul P. Aiello • Rosa, Pat, Nicolette, Francesco, and Marco Luisi •
Roseanne Milazzo • Rosina • Samantha Ho and Family • Sarah and Luis Lucero •
Silia, Todd, Samantha, and Alexandra Bailey • Susan and Mario Vilardi • Tara Kolton •
The Crane-Moscowitz Family • The Dunne Family • The Grasso Family • The Landa Family •
The McBrayer Family • The O'Brien Family • The Pennisi Family • The Salerno Family •
Tui Sutherland • Vishal Patel • Wayne Lopez

This story was originally written for Charles Anthony Zorger.

# Louisa Luisi

Louisa Luisi is an author and English teacher who has been writing and studying words for a very long time. She holds a BS in Education & English and a MA in English Education. She is the author of a number of plays that have been performed in New Jersey and New York City. Louisa writes, teaches, and lives in New Jersey. Visit www.LouisaLuisi.com for more information.

AUTHOR

LOUISA LUISI

# Kika Esteves

Kika Esteves is a Brazilian illustrator and comic artist. She was born in 1979 and graduated with a degree in Marketing and Advertisement Studies. She lives in Natal with her caring husband and two yellow cats. She could never understand why she had to grow up and to feed the child inside her, she dedicates her time to creating pictures for children's books.

ILLUSTRATOR

KIKA ESTEVES

# Be a part of our team!

Draw yourself in this baseball
card or paste a real photo in
the space below.

# Guess Who?

Guess the famous baseball players
who were given these nicknames.

Mr. October

_ _ _ _ _ _ _ _ _ _ _ _ _ _

The Ryan Express

_ _ _ _ _ _ _ _ _ _ _ _ _ _

The Big Unit

_ _ _ _ _ _ _ _ _ _ _ _

A-Rod

_ _ _ _ _ _ _ _

The Iron Horse

_ _ _ _ _ _ _ _ _ _ _ _

## Iron Man

_ _ _ _ _ _ _ _ _ _ _ _ _ _ _ _

## The Babe

_ _ _ _ _ _ _ _ _ _ _ _ _ _ _ _

## Hammerin' Hank

_ _ _ _ _ _ _ _ _ _ _ _ _ _ _ _

## The Mick

_ _ _ _ _ _ _ _ _ _ _ _ _ _ _ _

## Donnie Baseball

_ _ _ _ _ _ _ _ _ _ _ _ _ _ _ _

# Who are your best coaches?
## Have them sign this baseball.